D1514832

The Perfect Christmas

The Perfect Christmas

More Than 40 Gifts
and Recipes for a
Homemade, Handmade Holiday

LORENZ BOOKS
NEW YORK · LONDON · SYDNEY · BATH

This edition published in 1997 by Lorenz Books
Lorenz Books is an imprint of
Anness Publishing Inc.
27 West 20th Street
New York, New York 10011

Lorenz Books are available for bulk purchase for
sales promotion and for premium use.
For details write or call the manager of special sales,
LORENZ BOOKS, 27 West 20th Street,
New York, New York 10011. (800) 354-9657.

ISBN 1 85967 515 8

Editors: Anne Magruder and Jo Wells
Production Editor: Alicia Cech
Photographers: Karl Adamson, James Duncan, Michelle Garrett, Nelson Hargreaves,
Amanda Heywood, Gloria Nicol, Debbie Patterson, Polly Wreford
Contributors: Fiona Barnett, Penny Boylan, Carole Clements, Roz Denny,
Stephanie Donaldson, Tessa Evelegh, Gilly Love, Sue Maggs, Terence Moore,
Andrea Spencer, Liz Trigg, Liz Wagstaff, Stewart and Sally Walton, Pamela Westland,
Emma Whitfield, Elizabeth Wolf-Cohen

Design: Blue Inc.

Printed and bound in China

1 3 5 7 9 10 8 6 4 2

Contents

INTRODUCTION

THE PULSE QUICKENS, THE HEART GLADDENS—IT'S THAT magical moment before sunrise when children all over the world are opening their eyes and racing to the Christmas tree. Stockings have been filled with toys and candy, presents have been wrapped and festooned with bows, and breakfast has been prepared but for steaming mugs of cocoa and coffee. Throughout the day families will open gifts, greet friends and sing carols, re-living favorite traditions handed down through the generations. *The Perfect Christmas* is a glorious celebration of all that makes Christmas linger in our memories, long after the last candle has been put out and the last ornament packed away. From flickering lights to garlands of popcorn and crimson cranberries, to mulled cider and spicy gingerbread, Christmas is a time for savoring life and taking things slowly, pausing to appreciate the countless ways in which you and your family enjoy the holiday season. This book is a practical sourcebook of recipes and projects the whole family can enjoy, making Christmas as enchanting as it can be.

—*Amy Wilensky*

Festive Food and Drinks

A CELEBRATION OF SEASONAL FAVORITES,
WITH MODERN FLOURISHES AND TIME–TESTED
STANDBYS TO DELIGHT THE PALATE

COCKTAILS

CHAMPAGNE COCKTAILS AND SPARKLING PUNCHES HAVE JUST WHAT IT TAKES TO WELCOME CHRISTMAS GUESTS. A bracing alcohol-free Cranberry Frost is an ebullient accompaniment to a late breakfast or leisurely brunch. When the main meal is to be served in the evening, the more spirited Kir Royale has the sparkle to set the scene as the family—or at least the adult members of it—gets into the swing of the Christmas festivities.

CRANBERRY FROST

Makes 10 servings

INGREDIENTS
½ cup superfine sugar
juice of 2 oranges
½ cup cranberry juice
5 cups chilled seltzer or
   club soda
2-3 tablespoons fresh
   cranberries, to garnish
fresh mint sprigs,
   to garnish

1 Combine the sugar, orange juice and ½ cup of water in a small saucepan over low heat and stir until the sugar is dissolved. Bring to a boil, and boil for 3 minutes. Set aside to cool. (The syrup can be made in advance and stored in a covered container in the refrigerator until you use it.)

2 Place the syrup in a chilled punch bowl, add the cranberry juice and mix well. Just before serving, add the seltzer and garnish with cranberries and mint sprigs.

KIR ROYALE

Makes 1 serving

INGREDIENTS
2 tablespoons crème de cassis
½ cup chilled champagne
orange slice, to garnish

Place the crème de cassis in a chilled champagne flute. Add the champagne and stir to combine. Garnish with an orange slice.

ICE FOLLIES

Add flair to cocktails and punches with stylish ice cubes. For colored ice, stir a few drops of food coloring into a pitcher of water before freezing the water in ice-cube trays, then harmonize the ice and the cocktails—use red ice in a pink drink, for example.

Freeze strawberries, raspberries, blackberries or melon balls in ice-cube

trays. Place the fruit in each section and then fill it up with water. As an experiment, try freezing small (nontoxic!) flowers or herbs in a similar way.

Stylish ice cubes make pretty drinks (above). Cranberry Frost (opposite) is a bracing punch.

𝒜PPETIZERS

𝓑ALANCE IS KEY WHEN PLANNING DIPS, SPREADS and snacks to serve with drinks. Whether you're preparing appetizers or a buffet for a cocktail party, make your selections as varied as possible. Quick dips and marinated vegetables are a good starting point.

SMOKED TROUT SPREAD

Makes 2 servings

INGREDIENTS
½ cup ricotta cheese
½ cup sour cream
1 cup smoked trout pieces,
    fine bones removed, flaked
2 tablespoons prepared
    horseradish
¼ cup chopped scallions
1 tablespoon chopped fresh
    dill or parsley
2 teaspoons or more fresh
    lemon juice
salt and freshly ground
    black pepper
trimmed radishes, to serve
black bread, to serve
onion slices, to serve

1 Combine the ricotta and sour cream in a food processor and puree. Transfer to a mixing bowl.

2 Fold in the trout, horseradish, scallions, dill or parsley, lemon juice and salt and pepper. Transfer the spread to serving bowls and chill.

3 Serve the spread with radishes, black bread and onion slices.

MARINATED CARROTS

Makes 8 servings

INGREDIENTS
1 pound carrots, peeled,
    trimmed and thinly sliced
about 1 cup fresh orange juice
1 tablespoon sugar
fresh or dried tarragon or mint
    leaves (optional)

Combine all the ingredients in a bowl and marinate overnight. Drain and serve.

HERBED STILTON

Makes 8 servings

INGREDIENTS
8 ounces Stilton or other
    blue cheese
4 ounces cream cheese
1 tablespoon port
1 tablespoon chopped fresh
    parsley
1 tablespoon chopped fresh
    chives or scallions
½ cup finely chopped walnuts,
    lightly toasted
salt and freshly ground pepper

1 Place the Stilton or other blue cheese, cream cheese and port in a food processor and blend until smooth.

2 Transfer to a mixing bowl and stir in the remaining ingredients.

3 Spoon into ramekins, chill and serve.

Crudités and vegetable garnishes embellish spreads such as Herbed Stilton and Smoked Trout.

HOT ARTICHOKE PASTRY PUFFS

Makes 24 servings

INGREDIENTS
FOR THE FILLING
1 tablespoon unsalted butter
⅓ cup all-purpose flour
⅓ cup light cream or half-and-half
2 tablespoons milk
salt and freshly ground black pepper
generous pinch of cayenne
1 can (8 ounces) artichoke hearts, drained well and finely chopped

FOR THE PASTRY
1 package (1 pound) frozen puff pastry, thawed
1 egg, beaten, for glazing

1 Melt the butter in a saucepan over medium heat. Stir in the flour and cook for 5 minutes. Stir in the cream and milk and season with salt, pepper and cayenne. Bring to a gentle boil and let boil,

COOK'S TIP
For a more flavorful morsel use anchovy- or almond-stuffed olives from a specialty foods store.

stirring constantly, for 3 minutes. Remove from the heat. Stir in the artichoke hearts and cool to room temperature.

2 Preheat the oven to 400°F. Roll out the puff pastry on a floured board to a thickness of about ⅛ inch. Using a 3-inch fluted cookie cutter, cut the pastry into rounds. Brush the rim of each round with beaten egg.

3 Spoon some artichoke filling onto the lower half of each round. Seal.

4 Brush pastry tops with egg. Bake on a cookie sheet for 18–20 minutes, until golden. Serve immediately.

CHEESE AND OLIVE BITES

Serve these delicious bite-size morsels chilled and speared with toothpicks.

INGREDIENTS
1 package (8 ounces) cream cheese, at room temperature
about 16 stuffed green olives
⅓ cup chopped walnuts, lightly toasted

1 In a mixing bowl, beat the cream cheese until soft. Mold generous teaspoonfuls of the cheese around each olive. Roll olives between your palms to form neat spheres.

2 Place the chopped walnuts in a saucer. Roll the coated olives in the nuts to cover them evenly. Chill for at least 1 hour before serving.

Hot Artichoke Pastry Puffs are served with cooling cherry tomatoes. Olives are surrounded by choux pastry puffs.

Watercress and Orange Soup

THIS HEALTHY AND REFRESHING SOUP IS EQUALLY GOOD SERVED HOT OR CHILLED.

Makes 4 servings

INGREDIENTS

1 tablespoon olive oil
1 large onion, chopped
2 bunches watercress, trimmed
grated rind and juice of 1
*   large orange*
1 vegetable bouillon cube,
*   dissolved in 2½ cups*
*   boiling water*
⅔ cup light cream or
*   half-and-half*
2 teaspoons cornstarch
salt and black pepper
heavy cream or yogurt,
*   to garnish*
4 orange wedges, to garnish

COOK'S TIP

**Wash the water-
cress only if really
necessary; it is
often very clean
when purchased.**

1   Heat the oil in a large nonreactive saucepan over medium heat. Add the onion and cook until translucent. Add the watercress, cover and cook for about 5 minutes, until the watercress is soft.

2   Add the rind, juice and bouillon. Cover and simmer for 15 minutes. Puree in a food processor.

3   In a bowl, stir together the cream or half-and-half and the cornstarch. Stir the mixture into the soup.

4   Return the soup to a boil over very low heat, stirring until just slightly thickened. Season to taste with salt and pepper. If serving chilled, transfer the soup to a mixing bowl, cover and refrigerate.

5   Serve the soup with a swirl of cream or yogurt and a wedge of orange to squeeze in at the table.

Christmas Salad

A LIGHT FIRST COURSE THAT CAN BE PREPARED AHEAD AND ASSEMBLED JUST BEFORE SERVING.

Makes 8 servings

INGREDIENTS
FOR THE CARAMELIZED
ORANGE PEEL
1 tablespoon superfine sugar
4 tablespoons cold water
4 oranges

FOR THE SALAD
Mixed red and green
*   lettuce leaves*
2 pink grapefruit
1 large or 2 small avocados,
*   pitted, peeled and cubed*

FOR THE DRESSING
6 tablespoons olive oil
2 tablespoons red wine
*   vinegar*
1 garlic clove, crushed
1 teaspoon Dijon mustard
salt and freshly ground
*   black pepper*

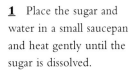

1   Place the sugar and water in a small saucepan and heat gently until the sugar is dissolved.

2   Remove the rind from the oranges, scrape away the pith and slice into fine shreds. Add to the sugar and water, raise the heat and boil for 5 minutes.

3   Dry the rind on a wire rack. Set the syrup aside to cool. You can make the recipe up to this point several days in advance.

4   Tear the lettuce leaves into pieces and set aside. Peel the grapefruit. Working over a bowl to catch any juice, cut the pith off the grapefruit and the oranges and segment them, removing all the pith and membrane.

5   Place all the dressing ingredients in a jar and shake until emulsified. Add the reserved syrup and adjust the seasoning. Arrange the lettuce and fruit on chilled salad plates with the cubed avocados and top with the dressing and the caramelized orange peel.

Shellfish with Seasoned Broth

Leave one or two mussels and shrimp in their shells to add a flamboyant touch to this elegant dish.

Makes 4 servings

INGREDIENTS

1½ pounds mussels, scrubbed
   and debearded
1 onion, thinly sliced
1 leek, thinly sliced
1 small carrot, julienned
1 garlic clove
4 cups water
pinch of curry powder
pinch of saffron
1 bay leaf
1 pound large shrimp, peeled
   and deveined
1 pound scallops
6 ounces cooked lobster meat,
   sliced (optional)
1-2 tablespoons chopped fresh
   chervil or parsley
salt and freshly ground
   black pepper

1 Place the mussels in a large, heavy soup pot or flameproof casserole and cover the pan tightly. Cook, shaking the pan occasionally, over high heat for 4-6 minutes, until the mussels open. Remove from the heat.

2 When the mussels are cool enough to handle, discard any that did not open. Remove all but 8 mussels from their shells, reserving a few for presentation, and set aside. Discard the empty shells. Strain the cooking liquid through a cheesecloth-lined strainer and set aside for later use.

3 Place the onion, leek, carrot and garlic in a large, heavy pot and add the water, reserved cooking liquid, spices and the bay leaf. Bring to a boil, skimming any foam that rises to the surface, then reduce the heat, cover and simmer gently for 20 minutes, until the vegetables are tender. Remove the garlic clove.

4 Add the shrimp, scallops and lobster meat, if using. After 1 minute, add the mussels. Simmer gently for about 3 minutes, until the scallops are opaque and all the shellfish is heated through. Adjust the seasoning. Ladle the soup into a heated tureen or shallow soup bowls and sprinkle with herbs.

COOK'S TIP

If desired, cook and shell the mussels and simmer the vegetables in the broth ahead of time. Then finish the soup just before serving.

Roast Turkey

For the stunning main attraction, serve this golden bird with Brussels sprouts and mashed potatoes.

Makes 8 servings

INGREDIENTS

FOR THE STUFFING

8 ounces lean bacon,
  chopped
1 large onion, finely
  chopped
1 pound bulk pork sausage
⅓ cup rolled oats
2 tablespoons chopped fresh
  parsley
2 teaspoons mixed dried
  herbs
1 large egg, beaten
⅔ cup dried apricots, finely
  chopped
salt and freshly ground
  black pepper

FOR THE TURKEY

1 turkey with giblets (about
  10 pounds, thawed
  overnight if frozen)
1 large onion, stuck with
  6 whole cloves
4 tablespoons unsalted butter,
  at room temperature
10 sausages

FOR THE GRAVY

2 tablespoons all-purpose
  flour
2 cups homemade giblet stock
  or turkey stock

1 For the stuffing, sauté the bacon in a medium, heavy frying pan until crisp. Pour off most of the fat, add the onion and sauté gently until the onion is tender and golden brown.

2 Transfer the sautéed bacon and onion to a large mixing bowl and stir in all the remaining stuffing ingredients. Toss well to combine thoroughly. Season well with salt and pepper.

3 Remove the giblets and neck bone and stuff the neck end of the turkey only. Tuck under the flap of skin and secure with a small skewer (do not overstuff the turkey or the skin will burst during roasting). Reserve any remaining stuffing.

4 Put the clove-studded onion inside the turkey and tie the legs together with twine. Place the turkey in a roasting pan. Adjust the oven racks to allow for the size of the turkey. Preheat the oven to 400°F.

5 Spread the butter over the turkey and season it generously with salt and pepper. Cover loosely with foil and cook for 30 minutes. Baste with the pan juices.

6 Reduce the oven temperature to 350°F and cook for 2 hours longer. Baste every 30 minutes. Remove the foil for the last hour of cooking and baste. The turkey is cooked if the juices run clear when the thickest part of the thigh is pierced with a skewer.

7 While the turkey is cooking, shape the remaining stuffing into small balls or pack it into a greased ovenproof dish.

8 About 20 minutes before the turkey is done, put the sausages in an ovenproof dish and bake for 20 minutes. Start the stuffing balls too, baking until golden brown and crisp, also about 20 minutes.

9 Transfer the turkey to a platter, cover with foil and let it rest for 15 minutes before carving.

10 To make the gravy, place the giblet stock in a medium saucepan over medium heat and bring to a simmer.

11 Spoon off the fat from the roasting pan, leaving the meat juices. Blend in the flour and cook over medium heat for 2 minutes. Gradually stir in the hot stock and bring to a boil. Adjust the seasoning and pour into a gravy boat.

12 Just before serving, remove the skewer and twine from the roast turkey. Pour any juices from the platter into the gravy. To serve, surround the turkey with sausages and stuffing balls. Carve at the table and serve.

COOK'S TIP

An alternate stuffing: combine stale corn-bread chunks with rendered bacon and sautéed onions and celery in a large bowl. Stir in chopped fresh sage, chopped pitted prunes, toasted hazelnut pieces, melted butter, turkey or chicken stock, salt and a generous grinding of pepper. Bake as directed.

Venison with Cranberry Sauce

*L*EAN AND LOW IN FAT, VENISON STEAKS ARE A healthy choice for a special occasion. Served with a sauce of fresh seasonal cranberries, port and ginger, they make a dish with a wonderful combination of flavors. If you wish, substitute pork tenderloin for the venison; it makes an equally festive main course.

Makes 8 servings

INGREDIENTS
1 orange
1 lemon
¾ cup fresh or frozen
  cranberries, picked over
1 teaspoon grated fresh ginger
1 thyme sprig
1 teaspoon Dijon mustard
¼ cup red currant jelly
⅔ cup ruby port
2 tablespoons vegetable oil
4 venison steaks
2 shallots, finely chopped
salt and freshly ground
  black pepper
thyme sprigs, to garnish
mashed potatoes, to serve
  (optional)
steamed broccoli, to serve,
  (optional)

1 Pare the rind from half the orange and half the lemon and cut it into very fine strips. Blanch in boiling water for about 5 minutes. Drain the strips and refresh under cold water.

2 Juice the orange and lemon and place the juices in a small saucepan. Add the cranberries, grated ginger, thyme sprig, mustard, red currant jelly and port.

3 Cook over medium-low heat until the jelly melts. Bring the mixture to a boil, stirring occasionally, then cover the pan and reduce the heat. Cook gently for about 15 minutes, until the cranberries are just tender.

4 Heat the vegetable oil in a large, heavy frying pan until hot but not smoking. Add the venison steaks and sauté over high heat for 2–3 minutes. Turn the steaks and add the chopped shallots to the frying pan. Cook 2–3 minutes longer, depending on whether you want to serve the venison rare or medium.

5 Just before the steaks are done, add the cranberry mixture to the frying pan, along with the lemon and orange rind. Bring the mixture to a boil and let simmer for a few seconds, until slightly thickened. Remove and discard the thyme sprig. Taste the sauce and adjust the seasoning.

6 Transfer the venison steaks to warmed individual serving plates and spoon the cranberry sauce over each serving. Garnish each plate with thyme sprigs and serve immediately with creamy mashed potatoes and steamed broccoli, if desired.

Salmon with Green Peppercorns

A FASHIONABLE DISCOVERY OF NOUVELLE CUISINE, GREEN PEPPERCORNS ADD PIQUANCY TO ALL KINDS OF sauces and stews. Available pickled in jars or cans, they are great to keep on hand in your pantry.

Makes 4 servings

INGREDIENTS
1 tablespoon unsalted butter
2 or 3 shallots, finely chopped
1 tablespoon brandy (optional)
¼ cup dry white wine
6 tablespoons fish or chicken stock (see Cook's Tip)
½ cup heavy cream
2-3 tablespoons green peppercorns in brine, rinsed
2-3 tablespoons vegetable oil
4 salmon fillets (about 6 ounces each)
salt and freshly ground black pepper
fresh parsley, to garnish

1 Melt the butter in a saucepan over medium heat. Add the shallots and cook for 2 minutes.

2 Add the brandy, if using, the white wine and the stock. Bring to a boil and continue boiling, stirring occasionally.

3 Reduce the heat to medium-low. Add the cream and half the green peppercorns, crushing them slightly.

4 Cook for 4–5 minutes, until the sauce is thickened, then strain and stir in the remaining peppercorns. Keep the sauce warm over low heat, stirring occasionally, while you cook the salmon.

5 In a heavy frying pan, heat the oil over medium-high heat until it just starts to smoke. Lightly season the salmon fillets with salt and pepper. Place the fillets in the frying pan and cook for 3–4 minutes, until the fillets are opaque throughout. The flesh should flake easily with a fork.

6 To serve, transfer the salmon fillets to warmed plates and top with the sauce. Garnish each serving with a sprig of parsley.

COOK'S TIP
To make a simple fish stock, place about 1 pound bones and trimmings (preferably from a mild white fish) in a stock pot with a chopped small onion, a chopped carrot and a chopped celery stalk, 6 white peppercorns and 6 whole cloves, a bouquet garni, a little dry white wine and 2–3 cups cold water. Simmer for 15 minutes only. If cooked too long the stock will be bitter. Skim foam. Strain.

LENTIL AND NUT ROAST

A N EXCELLENT CELEBRATION DISH THAT CAN BE served with all the trimmings, including vegetarian gravy. Garnish it with fresh cranberries and parsley sprigs for a really festive effect.

Makes 6–8 servings

INGREDIENTS
⅔ cup red lentils
1 cup hazelnuts
1 cup walnuts
4 tablespoons unsalted butter
1 large carrot, minced
2 celery stalks, minced
1 large onion, minced
4 ounces mushrooms, minced
2 teaspoons best-quality
  curry powder
2 tablespoons ketchup
2 tablespoons Worcestershire
  sauce
1 egg, beaten
2 teaspoons salt
4 tablespoons chopped
  fresh parsley
⅔ cup water
Vegetarian Gravy

1 Soak the lentils for 1 hour in cold water to cover, then drain well. Grind the nuts in a food processor until fine but not a paste. Set aside.

2 Melt the butter in a frying pan. Add the vegetables and sauté over medium heat for about 5 minutes, until softened. Add the curry powder.

3 Combine the lentils, nuts, vegetables, ketchup, Worcestershire sauce, egg, salt, parsley and water.

4 Grease a baking pan and line it with waxed paper. Press the lentil mixture into the prepared pan. Preheat the oven to 375°F.

5 Bake the roast for about 1¼ hours, until just firm. Cover with a sheet of aluminum foil if the top starts to burn.

6 Let the roast rest for 15 minutes before turning it out onto a serving platter and peeling off the paper. Serve immediately with Vegetarian Gravy.

VEGETARIAN GRAVY

Make a large batch and freeze it in small containers, to reheat and serve as necessary.

Makes about 2 pints

INGREDIENTS
6 tablespoons vegetable oil
1 large red onion, sliced
3 turnips, sliced
3 celery stalks, sliced
4 ounces mushrooms, trimmed
  and halved
2 whole garlic cloves
6 cups vegetable stock or water
3 tablespoons soy sauce
salt and freshly ground black
  pepper
generous pinch of sugar

1 Heat the oil in a large saucepan over medium-high heat. Add the onion, turnips, celery, mushrooms and garlic. Cook, stirring occasionally, until well browned, 15–20 minutes.

2 Add the stock or water and soy sauce and bring to a boil. Cover and simmer for another 20 minutes.

3 Puree the vegetables by rubbing them through a sieve with the back of a wooden spoon. Add a little more stock or water, and return to the pan.

4 Season to taste with salt and pepper. Add the sugar. Freeze at least half the gravy for future use.

Two Vegetable Side Dishes

THESE ENCHANTING VEGETABLE MÉLANGES MAKE EXCELLENT ACCOMPANIMENTS TO MEATS SUCH AS ROAST TURKEY.

BRAISED RED CABBAGE WITH APPLE

Makes 6 servings

INGREDIENTS

1 small red cabbage (about 2 pounds), quartered and cored
2 medium red onions, halved and thinly sliced
2 Red Delicious apples, peeled, cored, halved and thinly sliced
1½ teaspoons caraway seeds
3 tablespoons brown sugar
3 tablespoons red wine vinegar
2 tablespoons cold unsalted butter, diced
salt and freshly ground black pepper

1 Preheat the oven to 400°F.

2 Slice the cabbage quarters thinly.

3 Place one-quarter of the sliced cabbage in the bottom of a flameproof casserole. Season with salt and pepper.

4 Add another layer of the cabbage. Sprinkle with caraway seeds and 1 tablespoon of the sugar. Layer one-third of the onions and apples on top.

5 Continue layering until all the ingredients have been used, ending with a layer of sliced cabbage.

6 Pour in the vinegar and dot the top with the butter. Cover and bake for 1 hour.

7 Remove the cover and continue baking until the cabbage is very tender and all the liquid has evaporated, about 30 minutes longer.

GLAZED CARROTS WITH SCALLIONS

Makes 6 servings

INGREDIENTS

1 pound baby carrots, trimmed and peeled if necessary
3 tablespoons unsalted butter
2 tablespoons honey
2 tablespoons fresh orange juice
1 bunch (about 8 ounces) scallions, trimmed and cut diagonally into 1-inch lengths, some of the green included
salt and freshly ground black pepper

1 Cook the carrots in boiling salted water or steam them until just tender, about 10 minutes. Drain if necessary.

2 Melt the butter in a large, heavy frying pan over low heat. Add the honey and orange juice and cook, stirring, until the mixture is smooth.

3 Add the carrots and scallions. Raise the heat to medium and cook, stirring occasionally, until the vegetables are heated through and glazed, about 5 minutes. Season with salt and pepper before serving.

Garlic Mashed Potatoes

$\mathcal{T}$HESE CREAMY MASHED POTATOES ARE PERFECT with all kinds of roasted or sautéed meats—and although it seems like a lot of garlic, the flavor is sweet and subtle when it is cooked this way.

Makes 6–8 servings

INGREDIENTS
2 garlic bulbs, separated into
cloves, unpeeled
8 tablespoons (1 stick)
unsalted butter
3 pounds baking potatoes
½-¾ cup milk
salt and white pepper

1 Bring a small saucepan of water to a boil over high heat. Add the garlic cloves and boil for 2 minutes, then drain and peel each clove with a sharp paring knife.

2 In a heavy frying pan, melt half the butter over low heat. Add the garlic cloves, cover and cook gently, stirring occasionally, for 20–25 minutes, until very tender and golden. Do not brown the garlic.

3 Cool the garlic and butter slightly and spoon into a food processor; pulse until smooth. Transfer to a bowl, press plastic wrap onto the surface and set aside.

4 Peel and quarter the potatoes, place in a large saucepan and add just enough cold water to cover them. Salt the water generously and bring to a boil over high heat. Cook the potatoes until tender.

5 Drain the boiled potatoes in a colander and work through a food mill or ricer or press through a sieve back into the saucepan.

6 Return to medium heat and, using a wooden spoon, stir the potatoes for 1 minute to dry them out. Remove from the heat.

7 Warm the milk gently until bubbles form around the edge. Add the butter and stir until melted. Gradually beat the milk, butter and pureed garlic into the potatoes, then season with salt, if needed, and a little white pepper.

Brussels Sprouts Chataigne

In this dish, Brussels sprouts are braised with chestnuts, which are very popular in the winter months.

Makes 4–6 servings

INGREDIENTS
½ pound chestnuts
½ cup milk
4 cups small, tender
   Brussels sprouts
2 tablespoons butter
1 shallot, finely chopped
2–3 tablespoons dry white
   wine or water

1 Score a cross in the base of each chestnut. Bring a saucepan of water to a boil, add the chestnuts and boil for 6 minutes. Remove a few chestnuts at a time.

2 Holding each chestnut in a paper towel, remove the outer shell with a knife and peel off the inner skin.

3 When all the chestnuts are peeled, rinse the pan. Return the peeled chestnuts to the pan and add the milk.

4 Add enough water to completely cover them. Bring to a simmer over medium heat and cook for 12–15 minutes, until just tender. Drain and set aside.

5 Remove any wilted or yellow leaves from the Brussels sprouts. Trim the root ends, but leave them intact, or the leaves will separate. Score a cross in the base of each sprout.

6 In a large, heavy frying pan, melt the butter over medium heat. Stir in the shallot and cook for 1–2 minutes, until just softened.

7 Add the Brussels sprouts and wine. Cook, covered, over medium heat for 6–8 minutes, shaking the pan occasionally and adding a little water if necessary.

8 Add the chestnuts. Cover and cook for 3–5 minutes, until the chestnuts and sprouts are tender.

CHRISTMAS PUDDING

T HE CLASSIC ENGLISH CHRISTMAS DESSERT. WRAP IT IN CHEESECLOTH AND STORE IT IN AN AIRTIGHT container for up to a year to allow the flavors to develop. Make several to give as gifts to friends and relatives.

Makes 6 servings

INGREDIENTS

1 cup all-purpose flour
pinch of salt
1 teaspoon ground allspice
½ teaspoon ground cinnamon
¼ teaspoon freshly grated
    nutmeg
1 cup vegetable shortening,
    such as Crisco, frozen and
    finely grated
1 apple, grated
2 cups fresh white bread
    crumbs
2 cups brown sugar
2 ounces slivered almonds
1½ cups seedless raisins
1½ cups currants
1½ cups golden raisins
4 ounces dried apricots
¾ cup chopped mixed candied
    citrus peel
finely grated rind and juice of
    1 lemon
2 tablespoons molasses
3 large eggs
1¼ cups milk
2 tablespoons dark rum
fresh holly sprigs, to garnish

1 Sift together the flour, salt and spices into a large bowl. Stir in the grated vegetable shortening and apple and other dry ingredients, including the grated lemon rind.

2 Heat the molasses until runny and pour into the dry ingredients.

3 In a separate bowl, combine the eggs, milk, rum and lemon juice and stir into the dry mixture.

4 Spoon the mixture into two medium-size earthenware bowls or pudding molds. If using bowls, cover the puddings with waxed paper, pleating the

paper to allow for expansion, and tie with string. If using molds, fill about two-thirds full and cover tightly with the lid.

5 Steam each pudding on a trivet in a large pot of boiling water for 10 hours. Replenish the water frequently (use boiling water) to keep the pots from boiling dry.

6 When ready to serve the pudding, steam for 3 hours. Cool slightly and turn out onto a serving platter. Garnish with holly.

> **COOK'S TIP**
> Let a pudding rest long enough for most of the steam to escape before unmolding it. Then it will be less likely to crack.

Oranges in Caramel Sauce

THE APPEAL OF THIS REFRESHING DESSERT IS ITS lightness after a heavy holiday feast. Made in advance, it is easy and convenient for entertaining.

Makes 6 servings

INGREDIENTS
6 large seedless oranges
½ cup sugar
5 tablespoons water

1 On a board, using a sharp knife, cut a slice from the top and the base of each orange. Cut off the peel in strips from the top to the base, following the contours of the fruit.

2 Slice the peeled oranges into rounds about ½ inch thick. Put the oranges in a serving bowl and add any juice.

3 With a sharp knife, remove the pith from a few pieces of the orange rind. Stack two or three pieces at a time and cut into julienne strips.

4 Half-fill a large bowl with cold water and set aside.

5 Place the sugar and 3 tablespoons of water in a small, heavy saucepan without a nonstick coating and bring to a boil over high heat, swirling the pan to dissolve the sugar. Boil, without stirring, until the mixture turns a dark caramel color. Do not let it burn.

6 Remove from the heat and, standing back, dip the base of the pan into the cold water to stop the caramel from cooking.

7 Add 2 tablespoons of water to the caramel, pouring it down the sides of the pan, and swirl to combine. Add the strips of orange rind and return the pan to the heat.

8 Simmer the orange rind over medium-low heat, stirring occasionally, for 8–10 minutes, until slightly translucent.

9 Pour the caramel and rind over the oranges, turn gently to coat and chill for at least 1 hour before serving.

Frozen Grand Marnier Soufflés

THESE SOPHISTICATED LITTLE DESSERTS ARE ALWAYS APPRECIATED AND MAKE A WONDERFUL END TO A MEAL.

Makes 8 servings

INGREDIENTS

1 cup superfine sugar
6 large eggs, separated
1 cup milk
½ ounce powdered gelatin,
    dissolved in 3 tablespoons
    cold water
2 cups heavy cream
¼ cup Grand Marnier

1 Tie a double collar of waxed paper around 8 ramekins. Put 6 tablespoons of the sugar in a bowl with the egg yolks and whisk until pale.

2 Heat the milk in a small saucepan until almost boiling and pour it onto the yolks, whisking constantly. Return to the pan.

3 Stir the mixture over low heat until it coats the back of a spoon.

4 Remove the pan from the heat. Stir the dissolved gelatin into the custard. Pour into a bowl and set aside to cool. Whisk occasionally until the custard is almost set.

5 Place the remaining sugar in a pan with the water and dissolve it over low heat.

6 Bring to a boil, and boil until it reaches the soft-ball stage (240°F on a candy thermometer). Remove from the heat. In a clean bowl, whisk the egg whites until stiff. Pour the hot syrup over the whites. Let cool.

7 Whisk the cream until it holds soft peaks. Add the Grand Marnier to the cooled custard and fold the custard into the egg whites, along with the whipped cream. Pour into the ramekins. Freeze overnight. Remove the collars. Let sit at room temperature for 30 minutes before serving.

Moist and Rich Christmas Cake

THE CAKE CAN BE MADE 4 TO 6 WEEKS BEFORE CHRISTMAS. DURING THIS TIME, PIERCE THE CAKE WITH A FINE needle and spoon on 3 tablespoons of brandy. Try to do this once a week, until decorating with the icing.

Makes 1 cake

INGREDIENTS
1⅓ cups golden raisins
1 cup currants
1⅓ cups raisins
4 ounces prunes, pitted
   and chopped
¼ cup candied cherries, halved
⅓ cup chopped, mixed candied
   citrus peel
3 tablespoons brandy or sherry
2 cups all-purpose flour
pinch of salt
½ teaspoon ground cinnamon
½ teaspoon grated nutmeg
1 tablespoon cocoa powder
1 cup butter
1 generous cup dark
   brown sugar
4 large eggs
finely grated rind of 1 orange
   or lemon
⅔ cup ground almonds
½ cup chopped almonds

TO DECORATE
4 tablespoons apricot jam
10-inch round cake base
1 pound almond paste
1 pound white ready-made
   fondant icing
1½ yards ribbon

1 The day before baking, place the dried fruit and brandy or sherry in a bowl. Cover with plastic wrap and let sit overnight. Grease an 8-inch round pan and line with a double thickness of waxed paper.

2 Preheat the oven to 325°F. Sift together the flour, salt, spices and cocoa powder. In a separate bowl, cream the butter and sugar; beat in the eggs. Stir in the rind, almonds and dried fruit.

3 Fold in the flour mixture. Spoon into the pan.

4 Level the top and give the cake pan a gentle tap to ensure even baking. Bake for 3 hours, or until a skewer inserted in the center comes out clean.

5 Cool the cake in the pan on a wire rack for 1 hour. Turn the cake out onto the rack, but leave the paper on, to keep it moist. When the cake is thoroughly cool, wrap it tightly in foil and store.

6 One day before serving, warm the apricot jam, then strain to make a glaze. Remove the paper from the cake and brush it with hot apricot glaze.

7 Cover the cake with a layer of almond paste, and leave to dry for 24 hours. Cover with a layer of fondant icing. Tie a ribbon around the sides.

8 Roll out the fondant and stamp out 12 small holly leaves with a cutter. Make one bell motif with a cookie cutter dusted with sifted confectioners' sugar. Roll small balls for holly berries. Dry on waxed paper for 24 hours. Decorate the cake with the leaves, berries and bell.

*S*EASONAL *D*ECORATING

TRANSFORM YOUR SURROUNDINGS—FROM
TABLETOP TO TREETOP AND VIRTUALLY EVERY
SURFACE IN BETWEEN—INTO A
CHRISTMAS WONDERLAND

$\mathscr{S}$PARKLING $\mathscr{T}$ABLE $\mathscr{T}$OPPERS

$\mathscr{A}$T CHRISTMAS, DRESS YOUR WINEGLASSES FOR dinner. Lace fine gold wire around them, and add jewel-laden golden stripes and strings of gold beads to create simple yet striking table decorations. Add a tablecloth festooned with glittery gold stars for a lavish yet understated effect.

JEWELED GLASSES

1 "Lace" fine beading wire around the stem and bowl of a pretty wineglass or champagne flute. Taking care not to break the delicate wire by over-handling it, tie it to secure it to the glass. Once you are satisfied with the position, add a spot of glue.

2 Stick a length of masking tape long enough to go around the glass onto a piece of cardboard and spray it with gold paint. Use a utility knife and metal ruler to cut it into thin strips. Attach a strip to each glass near the rim, and trim with a stick-on jewel. Wash these delicate glasses by hand. If you lose some of the decorations, apply new ones.

YOU WILL NEED
fine beading wire
stemmed glasses
all-purpose glue
masking tape
cardboard
gold spray paint
cutting mat and knife
metal ruler
stick-on jewels
white voile to cover a table
artist's brush
gold paint

STARRY DRAPE

1 Place a circular object on a piece of cardboard and trace around it. Draw 3 lines for the star to make 6 equal sections.

2 Place the drawing under the voile and use an artist's brush to trace the star onto the cloth with gold paint. Repeat randomly over the entire tablecloth. Dry thoroughly.

Cinnamon Advent Candle

Advent candles often have calibrations along their length to tell you how much to burn each day during the countdown to Christmas. This unusual advent candle has a novel way of marking the passage of time: a spiral of 25 cinnamon sticks, each of decreasing height. Every day, the candle is burnt down to the next cinnamon stick, until finally, on Christmas Day, it is level with the shortest. For a heady bonus, the heat of the burning flame releases the spicy aroma of the cinnamon. Dried red roses complete the festive look of the candle. Remember, never leave an advent candle – or any candle – burning unattended.

1 Attach the cinnamon sticks to the outside of the candle by strapping them on with raffia as shown.

2 Position the cinnamon sticks in equal height reductions so that they spiral around the candle from the highest at the top to the shortest at the bottom. (It should cover about 2¼ inches of the candle.)

3 Cut the excess lengths of cinnamon from the sticks so that they are all flush with the base of the candle.

4 Once the base is level, push the cinnamon-wrapped candle into the center of the plastic foam ring. Make hairpin shapes from the .71 wires and pin the reindeer moss to the foam to cover the ring.

5 Cut the stems of the dried roses to a length of approximately 1 inch. Add a little glue to the bases and stems of the roses. Push them into the plastic foam through the reindeer moss to create a ring of rose blossoms around the candle.

YOU WILL NEED

25 medium-thickness cinnamon sticks

1 candle, approximately 3 x 9 inches

raffia

scissors

plastic foam ring for dried flowers, 4 inches in diameter

.71 wires

reindeer moss

20 dried roses

glue

Golden Place Cards

*T*OUCHES OF GOLD WILL TURN ORDINARY SMALL, ROUND-CORNERED CARDS AVAILABLE FROM STATIONERS into seasonal place cards. If gold doesn't fit into your design scheme, you can create equally lavish place cards with silver paint and pens. Gilded sprigs of fresh rosemary or pine would release a delightful seasonal scent. In addition to designating places at the table, these graceful cards can be used to label foods at a buffet dinner.

1 Score across the midway point of the card using a ruler and craft knife and fold it. Write the guest's name on the front in gold, and add a stick-on jewel, if desired.

2 Paint the leaves on the stems of foliage with gold paint. For a mottled, aged effect, lift off some of the excess paint with a dry sponge. Allow to dry.

3 Use the gilded foliage stem to decorate the card. (Remember, when working with gold, less is more. For an elegant place card, use gold sparingly.) After positioning, attach with glue. Dry flat.

YOU WILL NEED

small, round-cornered cards

ruler

craft knife

cutting mat

gold pen

stick-on jewels (optional)

gold paint

small artist's brush

stems of foliage

soft sponge

all-purpose glue

Silk Purse Tree Ornaments

*R*IBBONS ARE AVAILABLE IN A GREAT RANGE OF widths and colors, and you need only a small amount of each to make these delicate little purses. Use contrasting colors for generous bows around the top.

> **YOU WILL NEED**
> an assortment
> of pretty ribbons
> in festive colors
> scissors
> pins
> matching thread
> needle
> fine gold cord
> polyester batting

1 Cut strips of ribbon long enough to make a purse when folded in the middle, allowing for the raw edges to be folded down at the top. To make a striped purse, stitch narrower lengths of ribbon together using a running stitch.

2 With the wrong sides together, sew up the sides of the purse.

3 Turn right side out and tuck in the raw edges. Stitch on a loop of fine gold cord for hanging and stuff lightly with batting.

4 Gather the top of the purse together and tie with another piece of ribbon, finishing with a colorful bow.

Heavenly Gold Star

COLLECT AS MANY DIFFERENT KINDS OF GOLD PAPER AS YOU CAN FIND TO COVER THIS SPARKLING STAR, WITH its subtle variations of texture. It makes an attractive wall or mantelpiece decoration, and it would look equally splendid at the top of the tree. Try this technique on other shapes as well – to make a gilded sphere or cone, for instance.

1 Tear different types of gold paper into scraps of different sizes. Try to make a good assortment.

2 Dilute the white glue with a little water. Paint it onto the back of a piece of gold paper and stick it to the star.

3 Paint some more glue over the scrap of paper to secure it to the star. Work all over the front of the star, using different papers to vary the texture and color. Make a loop of wire and stick the ends into the back of the star for hanging. Secure with masking tape.

4 Cover the back of the star with different kinds of gold paper.

5 Let the glue dry thoroughly, then cover the star with a coat of gold glitter.

YOU WILL NEED
assorted gold papers (candy wrappers, metallic crepe paper, gift-wrap, etc.)
white glue
paintbrushes
styrofoam star
fine wire
masking tape
gold glitter paint

Exotic Ornaments

*T*HESE SEQUINED AND BEADED BALLS LOOK LIKE A COLLECTION OF PRICELESS FABERGÉ TREASURES, YET they're simple and fun to make. Hang them on the tree or stack them in a dish for a show-stopping decoration.

1 Make a template by cutting a paper circle large enough to completely cover the ball. Pin the netting to the template and cut it out. If desired, cut lengths of gold braid and pin around the ball to make a framework for your sequins.

2 Secure the netting to the ball using tiny pieces of tape. Don't worry if it looks a little messy; the tape and raw edges will be hidden later with sequins.

4 Thread a bead and sequin onto a brass-headed pin and gently press into the ball. Repeat until you have the number of designs required.

CRAFT TIP

When working out your designs use simple, repeating patterns and avoid using too many colors at a time on a single design.

3 Attach a loop of gold braid to the ball with a brass-headed pin.

YOU WILL NEED	
silk-covered styrofoam balls	tape
paper for template	brass-headed pins, ½ inch long
scissors	small glass and pearl beads
pins	sequins in a variety of shapes and colors
gold netting	
gold braid	

Gilded Nuts

Nuts are ideal subjects for gilding, because they have so much texture and detail and can be put to all sorts of decorative uses. They would make sumptuous table decorations for the Christmas feast or look lovely attached to gift boxes. Fill a few crystal bowls with gilded nuts and place them around the house to lend a feeling of seasonal splendor. Remember, when using any paints or varnishes, it is essential to keep your work area well ventilated. Work outside, if possible.

3 Wrap each sized nut in a sheet of Dutch gold metal leaf. Make sure that the nuts are completely covered, with no recesses or details exposed. Don't worry if it looks messy at this point; burnishing will smooth it out.

4 Burnish with a burnishing brush or soft cloth to remove the excess leaf. Seal with a thin, even coat of amber shellac varnish and let dry for 30 minutes to 1 hour. Once dry, the gold covering should be handled carefully as it is very delicate.

1 Cover a wide, well-ventilated area with old newspaper or heavy construction paper. Spray the nuts with red oxide primer. Be sure to coat them well. Let dry for 30 minutes to 1 hour.

2 Paint a thin, even coat of water-based size on each of the nuts, taking care to cover the ridges and recesses. Let the nuts sit for 20–30 minutes, until the coating becomes clear and tacky.

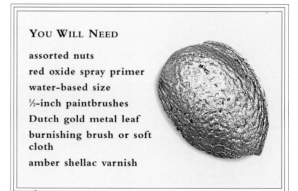

YOU WILL NEED

assorted nuts
red oxide spray primer
water-based size
½-inch paintbrushes
Dutch gold metal leaf
burnishing brush or soft cloth
amber shellac varnish

Classic Orange and Clove Pomander

*T*HIS CLASSIC POMANDER STARTS AS FRESH MATERIAL THAT, AS YOU USE IT, DRIES INTO A BEAUTIFUL, old-fashioned decoration with a warm, spicy smell evocative of mulled wine and the festive season. Make several pomanders using different ribbons and display them in a bowl, hang them around the house, use them as tree decorations or even place them in your closet.

Dried oranges make a decorative and sweet-smelling pomander when piled high in an attractive earthenware bowl.

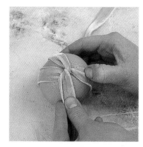

1 Cut a length of ribbon to fit around an orange twice with enough left to tie a bow. Tie it around the orange, crossing over at the base. (Don't pin at the base.)

2 Finish off at the top of the orange by tying the ribbon into a bow. Adjust the position of the ribbon as necessary to ensure that the orange is divided into 4 equal-sized areas. (You'll have to adjust the ribbon as the orange dries.)

3 Starting at the edges of each of the areas, push the sharp ends of the cloves into the orange skin. Continue studding with the cloves until each quarter is completely covered.

YOU WILL NEED

several small firm oranges

a few types of ribbon

scissors

cloves

Clementine Wreath

*T*HIS VIVID WREATH WILL LOOK SPECTACULAR HUNG ON A DOOR OR WALL. SET ON ITS BASE, IT CAN ALSO BE USED as a table decoration with a large candle in the center, or perhaps a cluster of smaller candles of staggered heights. The wreath is very easy to make, but it is heavy. If it is to be hung, be sure to attach it securely.

1 Push a length of .71 wire across and through the base of a clementine from one side to the other, and bend the 2 projected ends down. Bend another .71 wire to form a hairpin shape and push the ends through the middle of the clementine so that the bend in the wire is sitting flush with the top of the fruit. Do the same with all the clementines. Cut all the projecting wires to a length of approximately 1½ inches.

2 Soak the plastic foam ring in water. Arrange the wired clementines in a tight circle on top of the plastic ring by pushing their 4 projecting wire legs into the foam. Form a second ring of clementines within the first ring.

3 Cut the pyracanthus into small berry and foliage clusters approximately 2¼ inches long. Push the stems into the outer side of the foam ring and between the 2 rings of clementines, making sure it is evenly distributed.

4 Cut the ivy leaves into individual stems measuring approximately 2¼ inches long. Push the stems of the leaves into the ring, positioning a leaf between each clementine.

> **YOU WILL NEED**
> .71 wires
> about 30 clementines
> plastic foam ring about 12 inches in diameter
> pyracanthus berries and foliage
> ivy leaves

HOLIDAY GIFTS

A COLLECTION OF ONE-OF-A-KIND
HOLIDAY GIFTS, WITH INNOVATIVE WAYS TO MAKE
MEMORABLE TREATS AND PRESENTS

CHOCOLATE TRUFFLES

THESE TRUFFLES, LIKE THE PRIZED FUNGI THEY resemble, are a Christmas specialty. They can be rolled in cocoa or nuts or dipped in chocolate. Use semisweet, milk or even white chocolate.

Makes 20–30 truffles

INGREDIENTS
¼ cup heavy cream
10 ounces semisweet
*   chocolate, coarsely chopped*
2 tablespoons unsalted butter,
*   cut into pieces*
2-3 tablespoons brandy
*   (optional)*

FOR THE COATINGS
1 pound semisweet, milk or
*   white chocolate*
cocoa
finely chopped pistachios or
*   hazelnuts*

1 In a saucepan, bring the cream to a boil. Remove from the heat and add the chocolate, stirring until melted. Stir in the butter and the brandy, if using. Strain into a bowl and let cool. Cover and chill for at least 6 hours.

2 Line a large baking sheet with waxed paper. Using a small ice cream scoop or 2 teaspoons, form the chocolate mixture into 20–30 balls and place on the paper. Chill if the mixture becomes soft.

3 To coat with chocolate, freeze the truffles for 1 hour. In a bowl, melt the chocolate over a pan of simmering water, stirring until smooth. Cool slightly.

4 Using a fork, dip the frozen truffles into the cooled chocolate one at a time, tapping the fork on the edge of the bowl to shake off the excess. Place coated truffles on a baking sheet lined with parchment paper and chill immediately. Wrap and store, chilled, for up to 10 days.

5 Finish the remaining truffles by rolling in sifted cocoa and chopped nuts. Chill, well wrapped, for up to 10 days.

Candied Fruit

*M*AKE THIS IN THE LATTER PART OF WINTER, WHEN THE NEW SEASON'S CITRUS FRUIT IS AVAILABLE. ANY SYRUP that is left over from the candying process can be used in fruit salads or drizzled over a freshly baked sponge cake. To preserve the flavor of each fruit, candy them separately. The same process may be used to candy lemons, limes and oranges.

CANDIED CITRUS PEEL

Makes about 1½ pounds

5 large lemons, limes and oranges, unwaxed
3 cups sugar, plus extra for sprinkling

1 Halve the fruit, squeeze out the juice and discard the flesh, but not the pith. Cut the peel into thin strips.

2 Place in a pan, cover with boiling water and simmer for 5 minutes.

3 Drain, then repeat step 2 four times, using fresh water each time, to remove any bitterness.

4 In a heavy saucepan, combine 1 cup water and the sugar; heat to dissolve the sugar. Add the peel and cook slowly, partially covered, until soft (30–40 minutes). Cool thoroughly; sprinkle with sugar.

CANDIED GINGER

Makes about 1½ pounds

12 ounces fresh ginger
1 cup granulated sugar
superfine sugar, for coating

1 Place the ginger in a saucepan. Cover with water, bring to a boil and simmer gently for about 15 minutes, until tender.

2 Drain the ginger thoroughly and peel when cool. Slice ¼ inch thick.

3 In a heavy saucepan, dissolve the granulated sugar in ½ cup water and cook, without stirring, over low heat until the mixture becomes syrupy, about 15 minutes. Add the ginger and continue to cook over low heat, shaking the pan occasionally to prevent the ginger from sticking, until the ginger has absorbed the syrup. Remove the cooked slices; place them on a wire rack.

4 When cool, coat the ginger slices with the superfine sugar and spread them out on waxed paper for 2–3 days, until the sugar has crystallized.

FESTIVE LIQUEURS

THESE ARE EASIER TO MAKE THAN WINES AND MAY BE made with a variety of flavors and spirits. All these liqueurs should mature for three months before drinking. Each recipe makes about four cups of liqueur.

PLUM BRANDY

1 pound plums, pitted (reserving 3 pits) and finely sliced
1 cup raw sugar
2½ cups brandy

1 Place the plums in a sterilized jar with the sugar and brandy. Crack the pits, remove the kernels and chop. Add to the jar.

2 Cover with a lid. Store in a cool place for 3 months, shaking every day for 2 weeks and occasionally after that.

FRUIT GIN

3 cups raspberries or black currants
1½ cups sugar
3 cups gin

Place the fruit in a sterilized jar. Add the sugar and gin and stir until well blended. Cover and store as for Plum Brandy.

BOTTLING LIQUEURS

Sterilize the chosen bottles and corks or stoppers for each liqueur.

When the liqueurs are ready to be bottled, strain, then pour into the bottles through a funnel fitted with a filter paper. Fit with the corks or stoppers and attach decorative labels to the bottles.

CITRUS WHISKEY

1 large orange
1 small lemon
1 lime
1 cup sugar
2½ cups whiskey

1 Using a sharp knife or a vegetable peeler, pare the rind from the fruit. Squeeze out all the juice, and place in a sterilized jar with the rinds.

2 Add the sugar and whiskey and stir until well blended. Cover and store as for Plum Brandy.

ROSE-SCENTED BAGS

A TRANSLUCENT, GOSSAMER FABRIC MADE into a simple bag and filled with scented rose petals is a delightfully feminine gift idea. Include a small bottle of rose essential oil, so the recipient can keep the flowers lightly perfumed for years to come.

1 Lay the 2 pieces of fabric, right sides together. Sew a seam around all 4 sides, leaving a 1¼-inch gap on one side. Turn the bag through this gap so that it is right side out.

2 Press all 4 seams and slip-stitch the small gap closed. About one-quarter of the way down the bag, run 2 lines of stitches across the width of the bag, about ¾ inch apart, to make a channel for the drawstring.

YOU WILL NEED

FOR A BAG ABOUT
6 X 8 INCHES
outer fabric,
14 x 9½ inches
lining fabric
pins
needle and thread
scissors
adhesive tape
length of coordi-
nating color
cord, about 16
inches
2 matching
tassels
dried scented
rose petals

3 Fold the bag along its side seams with the right sides together. Sew up the bottom and side of the bag (by hand or with a sewing machine). Turn right sides out and press flat.

4 At the side seam, make a small snip in the outer fabric to allow the drawstring through. Wind a piece of adhesive tape around the end of the cord to prevent it from fraying and feed it into the gap in the seam. Feed it all the way around the bag and out at the other side through another small hole. Tie a single loop in each end of the cord and attach a matching tassel.

5 Fill the bag with scented rose petals. Pull the cord to create gathers in the neck of the bag. Tie a knot to secure the bag and neaten any edges.

Velvet Stocking

*T*HIS STOCKING IS SO ELEGANT THAT IT'S JUST ASKING TO BE FILLED WITH EXQUISITE TREATS AND PRESENTS. Use sumptuous fabrics in rich, dark colors for a sophisticated effect.

1 Copy the template for the cuff and increase to the size required. Place the template against a folded edge of the gold satin. Pin and draw around the pieces with tailor's chalk. Cut out 2 cuffs, leaving a narrow seam allowance.

2 Make a template for the stocking. Divide into 3 sections. Place the template for each section on a double thickness of each color of velvet. Pin and draw around each piece with chalk. Cut out, leaving a narrow seam, and pin together.

3 Once the 3 sections of velvet and the gold cuff for each side have been pinned together, machine-stitch each seam and clip any loose ends of thread.

4 On the right side of each piece of the stocking, pin a strip of decorative braid and a row of sequins. Sew on each by hand.

5 With right edges together, machine-stitch the 2 sides of the stocking together. Turn through, then fold down the gold satin outside to form a deep cuff.

6 Turn in the raw edges of the cuff and machine-stitch down to neaten, catching it to the seam of the velvet stocking.

7 Trim the gold satin cuff with a few gold buttons and stitch on a loop of decorative braid for hanging the stocking from a mantel.

YOU WILL NEED

paper	sewing machine
scissors	matching thread
gold satin fabric	decorative braid
pins	sequins
tailor's chalk	gold buttons
dress-weight velvet in three colors	sewing needle

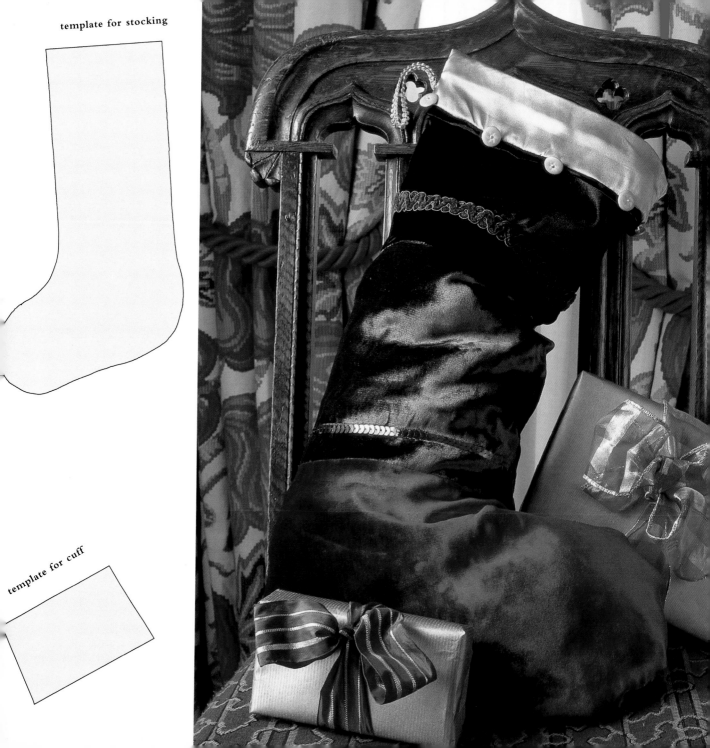

template for stocking

template for cuff

Star Printed Wrapping Paper

Complete an original gift by dressing it up with original, hand-decorated wrapping paper that's not only stylish but fun to make. This star pattern printed in festive colors makes great Christmas wrapping. Silver on blue is also an elegant combination.

YOU WILL NEED

cardboard or heavy paper for template

scissors

chalk

plain sheet of wrapping paper, preferably a matte

brown craft paper

star-shaped rubber stamp, in one or more sizes

red, green, white and gold latex paint

artist's brush

1 Cut a circular template out of cardboard and trace around it in chalk onto the wrapping paper, spacing the circles evenly on the sheet.

2 Print perimeters of alternate circles with red and green stars, brushing the paint evenly onto the stamp between each print.

3 Print white stars in the middle of each chalk circle, between the circles and in each corner of the wrapping paper.

4 Following the chalk circle between the stars, make rings of gold dots and dot the point of each star with gold.

Natural Gift Wraps

Even the most basic brown wrapping paper can take on a very special look. Use a gilded skeletonized leaf and gold twine in combination with brown paper. Coarser string would give a more robust look.

FILIGREE LEAF WRAP

This beautiful wrap is a clear case of lily-gilding.

1 Rub Treasure Gold into the skeletonized leaf.

2 Wrap a gift in brown paper and rub Treasure Gold onto the corners.

3 Tie the package with gold twine, bringing the ends together and making a knot. Fray the ends to create a tassel effect. Slip the leaf under the twine, securing it with glue at each end if it seems necessary. The leaves are delicate, so keep the gift clear of other packages once under the tree.

FRUIT AND FOLIAGE WRAP

Here, gilded brown paper provides a fitting background for a decoration of leaves and dried fruit.

1 Wrap the package with brown paper and rub in Treasure Gold, paying special attention to the corners.

2 Tie the parcel with seagrass string, then glue a different dried fruit or leaf to each quarter.

YOU WILL NEED

Treasure Gold

large skeletonized leaf

brown paper

tape

gold twine

hot glue gun and

glue sticks, if necessary

seagrass string

dried fruit slices, such as apples and oranges

preserved leaves

Star Painted Candle Holder

THE GENTLE GLOW OF CANDLES HAS AN OBVIOUS AFFINITY WITH STARLIGHT, AND THIS 12-POINTED STAR IS GILDED and studded with copper to reflect light. Painted in warm, festive colors, this holder would make a lovely addition to a traditional Christmas table.

1 Using a compass, draw a large circle on the plywood. With the same radius, mark the 6 points of the star around the circle and join with a ruler and pen. Draw a smaller circle on the pine and mark out the second star in the same way. Draw a circle in the center to fit your chosen candle size.

2 Cut out the two star shapes and sand any rough edges. Stick together with wood glue to form a twelve-pointed star.

3 Paint with white primer and sand lightly when dry. Cover with a base coat of dark green acrylic paint, then paint on the design. Seal with a coat of matte varnish.

4 Using the nail, make 6 holes for the copper disk rivets. Trim the stems of the rivets with wire cutters and push into the holes.

You Will Need	
compass	paintbrushes
¼ inch birch ply-wood sheet	white primer
ruler	acrylic paints in dark green, red and gold
pen	matte varnish
½ inch pine	large nail
fret saw	six ¼-inch copper disk rivets
sandpaper	wire cutters
wood glue	

INDEX

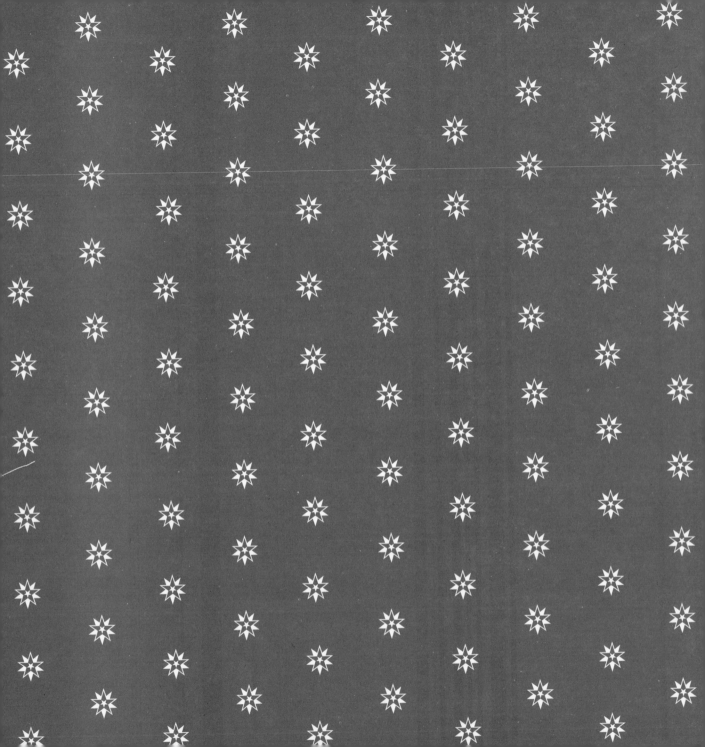